I breathe in

I breathe in

Poems of loss, love & hope

JULIE SALT

Published in the UK

Copyright

First paperback edition June 2020
Published by Julie Salt, Salted Press,
Shaldon Lodge, High Street, BH16 6BJ

Cover design: Rebekka Mlinar

Cover painting:
'HEAVEN IS PLACE ON EARTH WITH YOU'
by Nemesh

A CIP record for this book is available in the British Library

ISBN 978-1-8380494-1-6 (Paperback)

I breathe in

'I breathe in air so full of promise'

I breathe in is the debut poetry collection of the British writer and poet, Julie Salt. Although its many themes have flowed throughout her lifetime, it took her a decade to write them into poems, while the book itself only came into a full state of consciousness during the final months of a master's degree.

I breathe in is divided into two parts: *Earthquakes* focuses on painful feelings of loss, ranging from grief and despair, to fear, anger and insecurity. By contrast, the *Mountains* poems, concerned with love and hope, aim to lift readers' spirits through themes of human connections, passion, inner strength, family and even occasional humour. The duality of the collection reflects both the poet's relationship with her deceased brother, who sits at the heart of this work, and the belief that life offers us a choice between the two opposing mental states of optimism or pessimism; that said, whatever your choice, the poet hopes you will find both connection and comfort within these pages.

Julie Salt describes the collection's diverse poetic form and styles as 'Free Confessionalism' in which autobiographical experiences are liberated, along with the poetic imagination, in order to express their own unique and universal truths.

I breathe in

Poems of loss, love & hope

JULIE SALT

For

my parents

and my brother in absentia

Preface

When I was just sixteen weeks old, my brother who was then four-and-a half, died suddenly from a brain tumour. It was just days before Christmas. Whether through an absorption of my parents' grief or a deep desire to understand what my baby brain could not, this experience attuned my life to death and its many forms of loss. It also impacted me later in ways I could never have imagined. Most of us will lose a loved one at some point and experience the magnitude of grief's emotions, which can manifest as depression or anger, fear, guilt or loneliness and you will find all of these expressed in this book and more - some unexpected. However, as a pre-articulate baby at that time, I had no words to express or understand the tragic event that had befallen my family.

Instead, it was through the process of writing and compiling this collection of autobiographical poems that I realised how a loss could continue to reverberate through a life like the aftershocks of an earthquake. Even if we have only experienced a trauma in early childhood, its effects can still impact us later without us even realising it. I don't believe I am alone in this. Such repercussions of loss initially presented in my youth as a profound sense of family devotion and duty, a compassionate desire to console my parents, and to achieve for two people: my brother and myself. Later, these 'aftershocks' morphed into cravings for freedom from family intensity, manifesting as a need to escape, even from the life I had spent years building. These impulses, combined with a sense of seeking something, or more specifically some*one*, missing in my life, led me into territories wiser friends might have well chosen to avoid, where a lake of guilt, anger, confusion and depression finally surfaced, even though I couldn't then comprehend why.

Only recently, after reading Battat Silverman and Brenner's excellent book *Replacement Children: The Unconscious Script* [1] have I finally understood how my parents' loss was also my own; that it had left behind a silent, absorbed chasm of unresolved grief within me. As a result, I can now see why my brother's death caused aftershocks for me later in my life as a wife, mother and journalist and, despite having a wonderful career and a great family, triggered experiences that generated many of the loss poems in the *Earthquakes* section. Their themes of fear, sorrow, guilt, anger, loneliness, family breakdowns, affairs, despair, and even feminist fury, will be familiar to many of us. Ultimately, they are all underpinned by a loss of some sort, whether it is of people, love, security, power, freedom, privacy, pride, normality, or even a loss of beloved pets. The poem 'Magnitude' mourns a 'loss of normal' in the face of a viral pandemic, appropriate as I write in 2020, although it was drafted just before Covid-19 surfaced. By contrast, the prose poem 'Hester' offers a furious feminist, outpouring ironically expressing the many reasons why my lost freedom as a woman, mother and wife means 'I cannot write a poem about my truth,' although it seems I finally did.

The American Confessional poets, Robert Lowell (1917-77), Sylvia Plath (1932-63) and Anne Sexton (1928-74), writing during the era in which I grew up, were among the first to write autobiographically about then taboo subjects, like sex, depression, relationships and death. Although, my poems are based on autobiographical experiences like theirs, I was too young to consciously possess the words to articulate my brother's death for decades. 'Plane for Santa' was the first poem I wrote as an adult to confront my feelings and although I consider it to be technically autobiographical, it neither employs the personal 'I' form, nor the free verse conventions of modern Confessional poetry. This is because I could only express the story's deeper 'truth' by coalescing the sparse facts of the event, as told by my parents, with the fiction of my imagination. The resulting poem is a singsong, child-like narrative, told at arm's length, then pierced through with the pain of adult reality.

My MA supervisor, Dr. Tom Masters, helped me to see how, in my eternal quest to comprehend my brother's loss and parents' bereavement, I repeat the theme from different perspectives by pushing the boundaries of the autobiographical poem; 'Shade' frames it by using my journalist's background to tell a story through the voice of a refugee who finds safety in New Zealand's Al Noor mosque, only to find his safe place suddenly violated and his young son dead. The parallels with my arrival as a baby into the safety of my parents' arms and the sudden loss of that safe place through my brother's death, resounds through this piece. You will find many poems in this collection shot through with such 'artistic licence' where words of fact and fiction merge to create their own unique, universal 'truths'.

By contrast, a therapist once described me as my parents' 'rescuer' and the *Mountains* section of this book represents that part of my psyche which desires, even feels compelled, to bring comfort and love to others when a world becomes shaky - a common trait among 'survivor siblings' according to Battat and Silverman[2]. Thus, the poems diverge here from the despairing themes of *Earthquakes,* to pour a salvo on pain and to inject optimism. Unlike some Confessional poets who chose death over life in both poetry and reality (Plath and Sexton both committed suicide), the reawakening and more joyful poems of *Mountains* ultimately rise to celebrate life and to remind us that kindness, human connections, hope and our inner strength always continue to exist; 'Woman' conveys this through friendship, 'Philosophy Falters' through passionate sex, and 'Single Bed' through childhood feelings of security. The book's title poem, 'I Breathe In' shows the body as a source of inner strength and happiness, while 'The Breath Connects Us' suggests we are never alone. Both poems show how the simple, mostly unconscious act of breathing links us equally to our past, present and future, to trauma, rapture and each other. The words for the latter poem came after I experienced an emotional response to a mindfulness meditation, when I realised my brother and I had both breathed the same air when he was alive from the moment I was born, and that the breaths I continue to breathe from then to this day, connect me directly to him and his time on earth. The overridingly comforting message of both these breath-related poems and indeed this entire collection, is one of choosing life over death, strength over sorrow, gratitude over grief.

The loss-to-hope transition also defines the collection's narrative arc, as it spirals first downwards through life-shattering 'earthquakes' of loss, to lead the reader back up to a higher 'mountain' plane where we can breathe in sweeter air. If 'earthquakes' didn't shake our lives, we could never appreciate the view from the 'mountains'; and all the while, our breath connects us through our experiences, and can calm us if we choose to let it.

The Transcendentalist writer, poet and philosopher, Ralph Waldo Emerson (1803-1882) once said:

> *'The imagination wakened brings its*
> *own language, and that is always*
> *musical. It may or may not have rhyme*
> *or a fixed metre; but it will always*
> *have its special music or tone.'*[3]

Likewise, you can expect the 'unique musicality' of the collection of poems in *I breathe in* to sing through many voices of poetic expression and the 'self'. Free verse exists certainly within these pages, but you will also find traditional meter, rhyme, humour and playful experimentation. Simply put, the poems speak for themselves. I call this form 'Free Confessionalism' and I hope its diversity will stimulate emotional responses of empathy and pleasure in equal measure to 'Make it New'[4] for a generation connected by its humanity and compassion. I hope too these poems will offer love and hope to all readers seeking solace in these unquestionably shaky times and at any other moments of difficulty, loss, pain or upheaval.

JS. Spring 2020

Acknowledgements

After what was an educationally life-changing year on a master's degree in Creative Writing and Publishing at Bournemouth University (2018-19), I'd like to thank my course leaders, Dr. Helen Jacey and Dr. Brad Gyori for their excellent guidance. I'd like to extend my gratitude also to my supervisors, Dr. Tom Masters and Emma Scattergood MA for their expert advice throughout my final major project which formed the foundations, as well as some of the 'Eureka!' moments, of this book.

I dedicate *I breathe in* especially to my brother, Anthony Salt in absentia, without whose life this work would not have come into existence. Eternal love and thanks to my parents, my inspiration for smiling through sadness and always living life to the full; also to my family, source of inspiration, support, feedback, formatting, logo-design and biscuits throughout this, sometimes arduous, literary journey. My thanks too to my dear friends, Joanne, Nabil, Tig, Vonny, Sian, Linda, Hawwah, Jonathan, Marianne, Charlotte, Tom, Mav, Chris and Ann K, and many more, who along with my family have continued to believe that I could one day write something of value to others.

In addition, I would like to acknowledge inspiration from the New Zealand poet, Tusiata Avia's work, 'I cannot write a poem about Gaza' which helped to birth my own poem, 'Hester'. My warmest thanks to the inspired artist, Nemesh, also in New Zealand, for allowing me to use his divine painting, 'Heaven is Place on Earth with You' on my cover and certainly last but not least, huge gratitude to my exceptionally talented and hard-working designer in Holland, Rebekka Mlinar. Between them both they have created a truly vibrant and global hug around these poems. Thank you one and all.

Contents

Preface   *xi*

Acknowledgements   *xvii*

Poems of Loss | **Earthquakes**

His Chelsea Boots   5

Atmos-fear   6

Insomnia   7

Shade   9

Plane for Santa   11

Gas Oven   13

Guilt Sponge   15

Piano Notes   16

Freeze Frame   17

Winds of Change   19

First Base: anger   21

Bonfire   22

Thread Needle   23

Family Shot – a Tritina   24

Caves Elsewhere   25

Standing Stone   26

The Time of My Life   27

Traffic Jam   28

Ghost   29

Found at Last!   31

Voodoo Spells   32

Hester   33

Square One   35

Ice and a Slice   36

Old Scarf   38

Bare Knuckle Fight   39

Nausea   40

Hill of the Dead   42

Bittersweet   44

Thus   45

Two-way Glass   47

Let Down   48

The Sigh   49

Missing-part Life   50

The Void   51

Canine Crater: haikus for my dog I   53

Acetylene   54

Magnitude I   55

Poems of Love & Hope | **Mountains**

Hope's Genesis	61
Woman	62
Spinoza Spirits	64
And Sunshine Helps	65
Tuesday Lunchtime	66
Venez May Day	68
Woodland Walk	69
Love's Sunrise	71
Ocean's Drop	72
Essence	73
Reclining on a Bench	74
Relentless	75
Gently	77
Philosophy Falters	78
The Spring	80
One Day	82
The Breath Connects Us	83
Fibonacci	84
Joy	85
Dark Skies	87
Dancing Daughter	88
Trembling Twelve-ling	89
Different	90

Locusts on Holiday   91

Birches   94

The Beach   95

Gold of Ages   97

The Swan: elegy for a dance teacher   99

Hands   101

Mousehole in May   102

Believe   103

Canine Crater: haikus for my dog II   105

On Solitude   106

I Breathe In   107

Love   109

Profound   110

Single Bed   111

Magnitude II   112

Please Review I breathe in   *115*

About the Author   *117*

Endnotes   *119*

I breathe in

Poems of Loss | **Earthquakes**

His Chelsea Boots

His Chelsea boots beneath the seat
     Soft, tan suede   creased by his feet

Warmed every day, worn every day
                    Walked every day

Now still.

Atmos-fear

next door are brushing up the yard
birds chatter soft upon the bough
fragrant air defines the hour

and the minutes they wind so slowly now

a plane on clouds and whispering trees
with cool and heady night-time leaves
curtains catch a cinnamon breeze

and the hours they grind so slowly now

cicadas chirp a low-pitched drone
anguish smells of lost cologne
of nicotine and sun-washed stone

and a tear rolls down so slowly now

no one hears me, no one's near
just darkness, heat, and atmosphere
i lay, clutched to my rigid fear

and the end it comes so slowly now

Insomnia

Silence
still, cold, sharp moonlight

Darkness
teeming with troubled thoughts
voices jabbering, of everything and of nothing

Ticking
life seconds slipping through the stillness

Ringing, in my ears
the blood runs rushing, still hurrying to catch up
with the life that was
but no longer is

Nothingness
full of unspoken pain and sorrow

Loss … of what was and is no more

Numbness
sweeter death than this!

waiting
waiting
waiting

white towelling, soft waffle dressing gown
reminder of childhood comforts
and life, once lusty-rich and gold-top good
but now my bedtime milk stands cold

subtler pens than mine can flourish
words that grow and care and nourish
but my winter garden all cut down
bears bleak soil and seeds of anguish
in dawn's grey, unenlightened gloom

green tips, which cautious, dared to peep
will fill no bed with perfumed sleep
for all their steadfastness and passion
they may phoenix-rise again
one lovely sun-filled March spring morn

but not I

Shade

my shining silent golden orb of tranquillity
rolled behind a cloud one day in summer
its radiance and warmth usurped by a
thunderous claustrophobic clamour

an oppressive air of doom and din breezed in
to fill each nook and chink
where once was light and sparkling dust
came hailing palls of callous cracks

my head and breath *knew* heavy air
as wartime storms forced me from home
but Christchurch gifted me Al Noor
and I'd knelt in peace beneath its dome

my shining silent golden orb of tranquillity
full disarrayed within a stream
for all the world to see therein
            the torrents   of that moment

shattering shots across the moors
lightning bolts that sought to smother
any souls who crossed their path
from praying dad, to child and mother

my ears astute to every beat, my
fingers crept to sense my son, whose
skin like lead and eyes face-down,
lay sleeping there   austere as stone

my shining silent golden orb of tranquillity
rolled behind a cloud one day in summer
when innocence unfurled its fronds
as one dark-lit view, laid shade on another

Plane for Santa

at Christmas time
all presents wrapped
the joyous angel sat aloft
the Christmas tree
all dressed in light
the fair-haired boy lay very quiet

the watchful parents
eyes aglitter
saw him draw
a plane for Santa

"Will it fly to Heaven Mummy?"

mother smiled and stroked his hair
father held her hand

four days before
the big day dawned
at ten past one
a phone call came.
father heard

"I'm sad to say your son just passed away."

on Christmas day
all presents wrapped
the hallowed angel sat aloft
the watchful parents
eyes aglitter
knew he took
the plane for Santa.

Gas Oven

it was a *Chambers*
the talk of their friends
with clotted cream doors
an elegant front
handles of stardust
all the dials you'd want
bought for their wedding
in 19 53

you'd never have thought it connected to me

but the gas in those days
could kill you straight out
and my mother, she knew it
and the seed thought, it grew
she'd do it that day
when the grief felt too raw
when the pain got too much

with my father at work
she opened the doors of the elegant front
knelt by the dials
turned on the gas
with a hiss it erupted awaiting a match
releasing its sweet child oblivion fumes

I was upstairs, asleep in my cot
and when I started to cry
my mum says   she stopped.
'I couldn't commit suicide,' she once told me.
'I had to take care of a newly born baby.'

she still says I bailed her
still calls me her 'saviour'
yes, the baby me saved her
        because my brother wasn't there

Guilt Sponge

Body in the boot
Wrapped in black plastic
Fragmented nightmare recurring
Is it you?
Or my guilt that resurges
in dark hidden dreams
Did I kill you?
My fault?

Or did I absorb this?
Sucked up like a sponge from our mum?
I,   The guilt sponge of her grief?
Her self-blame when you left?
When you left her
and Dad.

Did I feel it was me?
Was I to blame too?
Only out of her body, mum's body, just weeks
still suckling her milk
Was I sipping her grief?
My first feelings of life
and of death
sapping joy from my birth
Was the guilt as much mine   as she felt it was
                                                    hers?

Piano Notes

breeze of piano
notes to ripple grief's surface
lost teardrops in waves

Freeze Frame

You rendered me to a freeze frame
a flat faced sepia smile
mocking anguish
permanently present
in this picture
and in the others left behind
all left behind

time, ticked its icicle tears
dripped from the day no one
wanted to remember
to a future no one
could imagine
they couldn't possibly imagine

You pinned me down to the past tense
a life-sentence
of obsessive revisiting
condemned to fend with the others
in a heart stopping torpor of
drowning souls, clamouring for life
clamouring, clamouring to breathe

You left me behind in transcendence
in the house no more a home
baby soft
whose future calls
for a new sentence
so I fill the void
with the present tense, the present tense – that's
now

You render me to a freeze frame
a flat faced sepia smile
locked-in anguish
permanently present
in this sister
and in the others left behind
all left behind

Winds of Change

Winds, winds of change, you're
smashing at my panes
Pawing lions roaring down the chimney to my
hearth
Disquieting, unsettling
Curtain-flags flap-flapping in
Seeking out the whiff of sin, you're
snuffing out the brightest fires, and blowing
chills back in

Flying in the face of the tallest standing twins
Hijacking the plane of Islam
Smoking out my clear horizon
Terrorising glass and tiling
Hurling fragile skin from buildings
Broadcasting the word to *shame*
A thinly masked excuse to maim, you're
whipping up a world of blame and blowing
fear back in

Crashing waves reverberating
Refugees, your naked threat
I'm powerless to stem the tide with
Nations losing amity
Flipping up democracy in
stormy seas of hate and maim, your
darkness, death's amphetamine, you're
drowning out the warmest wills and blowing
war back in

Decapitating hurricane
The World News brings you in again
My quaking heart just wants to block your
Demon barbers splitting heads, condemning
flesh to earth and dread
Your martyrs' wills strike shudders in me, your
fetid breath blows out to scare me,
Extinguishing angelic flames and blowing
death back in

First Base: anger

Fist face
Grist brow
Neck twists towards a rowdy
Shoulders hunch
like moss-spilled bough
Like moss-spilled bough spells danger
first base: anger
is no stranger
No stranger
but your first base: anger
just kills me

Bonfire

tongues of flame languish
licking heart sore wounds
wagging in the winds of infernal out breaths
their pulsing passions perform
in a hellish, headstrong, blazing bonfire

acrid tang on licking lips
spitting vitriolic vipers
sharp, stinging, forking lightning-tips
vile friends
of this hellish, headstrong, blazing bonfire

gnawing, nagging, angry zest
seething, down-turned bitter lips
heart full, hateful, hurtful Hell-fuel
burns white hot
within the hellish, headstrong, blazing bonfire

sharpest in-breaths sense the smoke screens
teary eyes screw up against
the caustic, claustrophobic cloak
that veils vastly heinous crimes
beneath my hellish, headstrong, blazing bonfire

fervent fingers jabbing air
fury shards enrage the flames
incensed, no sense, engulfed in loathing
until we're ashes all
from our hellish, headstrong, blazing bonfire

Thread Needle

Jabbing me into a deadly black hole
Spitting me out with your vitriol!
Dismissing me, yet you're missing the point

I ask how it is   that
'our assets are *joint?*'

£

Joined at the hip or bound by a slip?
Sweet words by the pond - or wads by the pound?
Your love sweeps me away on a 'maximize' tide

whose ensuing tsunami drowns out
my voice army

£

Bank of England stone sergeant bellowing orders
Commanding his minions to 'Buy!' and to 'Sell!'
Commits this Old Lady who's threading her needle,

to save every stitch, just in time.
Rot in Hell!

£

The fabric between us is ripping apart
For filthy damn lucre has captured your heart
Sew your silks for an empire of ingots and splendour!

But lose all, for the want of a word
that was tender

Family Shot - a Tritina

Vine arms entwined for the perfect photo:
Who'd doubt we were a flawless family?
Ear-to-ear smiles   pure magazine snapshot!

But look closer up - Mother's eyes are bloodshot.
She found out secrets through telephoto
lenses   so Father fist-ruled his family;

condemned and ridiculed this family.
Mum's sweet-Lisa smiles gagged truth like gunshot.
The camera never lies, but a photo?

This photo, it shows   a family shot.

Caves Elsewhere

In caves elsewhere you sought your shelter
You Gigolo! Lothario!
You wanderer! Philanderer!
Never home   your home was me
You never saw what I could see

'See this letter? Have I lost you?
She has your child inside her womb!
Will you leave me? Have you left me?'

'I told you that would never happen…'

'Do you love me? Do you want me?'

'Yes, I do, our contract stands. Till Hell freezes
over…truly.'

A burning heart in Arctic hands
Pregnant pauses, stormy silence
Icehouse princess riding high

A baby born
Court battle won
A home torn down
Patriarch gone

In caves elsewhere you sought your shelter
You wanderer! Philanderer!
Never home   your home was me
You never saw what I could see

Standing Stone

a standing stone
stood solitary in a stormy sea
all around
swirling tides
eroded her emotion

the single rock
exhaled no pain as vultures' claws took hold
digging in and taking off
they left the statue
cold

the monolith
bore the brunt of all the selfish waves
holding fast
erect and proud
a slave to nature's knaves

The Time of My Life

standing at the sink again washing up the pans again
kneeling at the washing machine pulling out black
socks
dragging out the vacuum cleaner sucking up the grime
flicking out the duster and dusting up
the time of my life

wishing i was washing on a golden sun-drenched beach
hanging out the socks on a makeshift washing line
three sandy-footed children hollering out a rhyme
running in and out among the dunes

kiss-soft evening breezes send ruffles through my hair
my face feels peachy-pink and my feet are freedom
bare
kindly waves are lapping and a beer is getting cool
time to sit and contemplate   time
to break some rules

wishing i was washing on a golden sun-drenched beach
but here i am trapped in my house and none of that in
reach
filling up my mundane hours sucking up the grime
flicking off the lustre and rusting up
the time of my life

Traffic Jam

It's a never ending pending as the pendulums tick-tock
Tramp… tramp… tramp, it's always now upon my
clock…

And nothing doing …

Endless restless urgency! I'm kicking up my heels!
To move from now to then and put some ground under
my wheels…

But here I sit … nothing doing …

Young voices cry out on the way, 'Mummy, are we
there yet?'
Old voices murmur at the end, 'Yes. There… we made it.'

So why not me?

My head demands each second, 'Did I miss a life
divine? Is today to stay?

…Or can I make tomorrow mine?'

Ghost

i've missed boyfriends and lovers — always

what if that 'missing'
was your ghost
come to me through our mum?
you left before i could speak
or walk or understand
but what if this endless missing, longing, yearning
feeling of
seeking of
something or
some*one*
missing
is what she passed to me
or projected maybe?

so, what if,
before i knew anything
while burbling on my baby back
watching, sensing, taking it all in
i absorbed all that missing, longing, grief and
yearning
to have him back
her beautiful boy
you, my brother?
and from the first time i ever loved a boy

i couldn't let it go
let *him* go
even when it was over
i felt that missing, longing, grief and yearning
i held a candle a long time for him
always
even when it made no sense
at all
was it your ghost? is it you calling?

Found at Last!

'I've found you *at last!*'
She typed so fast
Her fingers keen to send her mail

Within a day he had replied,
'I'm over the moon to hear from you.
I never thought we'd write again.
How the devil *are* you?'

Her fingers still so swift and warm
She told him how his mail
Had made her heart beat pounding fast
But, did his ardour still prevail?

In reply he said it did,
But added that her mother
Back in the day had warned him off
To cease from being her lover

How her jaw dropped!

She never knew
It made her feel so dismal sad
It was not right!
She thought he'd gone

So, she'd spent her life with another

Voodoo Spells

lustful lips cast voodoo spells
'but I'm a wife, you know,' she smiled.
'so… what do you want from me?
what *could* you want from me?'

noontime laughter, champagne shared
lashes lifted, not so coy,
sweet kissed cheeks, her shyness slain,
sunshine secrets. *perfect day*

a ballet-tender secret life,
a stealthy thief, a stolen wife
in portobello red-wine bistro,
longing lips purred whispered words

'I am yours'
'and you are mine.'
'as one forever.'
'love sublime.'

though guilt fought lust in nuptial bed
and gold was wrung on married hands
the voodoo magic had its way
Not one could leave. Nor could they stay.

a russian wedding ring his troth
zhivago tri-part bands their meld
inscribed inside accepting angst
'in three forever we are held'.

Hester

I cannot write a poem about my truth because I cannot swallow an entire earthquake.

I cannot write a poem about my truth because if I swallow an entire earthquake there'll be no room for the rest; my belly will be full of nausea, bile, and vomit and my pockets will be empty.

I cannot write a poem about my truth because if I speak out, you'll state I'm irresponsible, irrational, hateful, hurtful; you'll call me 'Hester' and force me to cut out cloth letters and sew them onto my top.

I cannot write a poem about my truth because the guilt I'll accept will raven out of my chest to peck out his eyes and mine, to cast us aside, blinded and bloodied, and meat-raw as rotting stiffs.

I cannot write a poem about my truth because even now a woman's place   is in the home, a woman's place   is with her kids, a woman's place   is with her husband, a woman's place   is caring for parents, a woman's place   is to do what is expected, what is expected, is expected of her.

And a man's is not.

I cannot write a poem about my truth because I hide behind respectability and shame and guilt and a beautiful apartment and shame and guilt and respectability - and fear.

I cannot write a poem about my truth because it's complicated, so complicated that I'd need to take a PhD in Law, Divorce law, Financial law, Property law, and Family Psychology, before I could even start again.

I cannot write a poem about my truth because it's an impenetrable Gilead republic, where even mates - yes, even those with guts cut out - would condemn me; not those neck-hanging by the city walls, of course, but for them, it's too late.

I cannot write a poem about my truth because I *can* do mathematics and the needs and desires of one entire family and one entire society, divided by the needs and desires of one single Hester, don't equate, especially when the Hester is a mother, a daughter, a wife, a woman, a lover.

I cannot write a poem about my truth because I'm afraid it'll set off an earthquake that'll carve a cleft through my entire house, setting my family, friends, finances, society, liberty, sanity and my stability, on the one side

and me on the other.

Inspired by 'I cannot write a poem about Gaza' Tusiata Avia [5]

Square One

Back to square one.
What was good
about us? Where did
we start? What made
us a pair? Shut my
eyes to recall what
we had. It's a blank.

What am I seeking?
I call to say… what?
I'm angry and hate
you or I'm sorry and
sad? I really don't
know. I'm hitting
a wall. I hang up.

Nothing comes back.
Have I blocked it all
out? What was good?
Did I love you? I
really don't know
and I really don't
care. What is love?

Not sure what is left
of me or of us. No
more back to square
one. It's only a
square. I came back to
the start but I found
nothing there.

Ice and a Slice

'Do you want ice?' Her date inquired.
She nodded warmly in reply.
Her eyes' Mariana depths
revealed her heart's desire.

'And a slice?' He continued unaware –
his brows arched
in expectation
with his hand.

He handed her
the icy slicey gin, so pricey,
turned and paid
and closed his wallet. Snap!

Her fingers clasped the Arctic glass.
So warm they were, it made the outside drip
with condensation.
This caused the girl to lose her grip.

She saw the silken, wetted vessel
sliding in slow motion from her satin tips.
He saw it too and pursed his lips
in some distant form of disapproval…
and vexation.

Glass hit floor and splinter splashed
into a million sparkling shards
of ice and slice
and pride and heart…
the liquid lost and never even tasted.

Their eyes met.
His, a steely, opaque blue,
the crevice in a glacier.

Hers, volcanic, warm and dark,
divulging depths he now
would never savour

'I'm so sorry!' She spluttered aghast.

He nodded tightly.
And called for the barman
to 'sort the mess'.

Old Scarf

when you've had enough of eyes that roll
in condescension and shit like that,
that sideways glance away from you
away from me,
actually

yes, I'm talking about me

when I've had enough of eyes that roll, because he's
talking down to me, a taste of sunlit days gone bad lolls
round my mouth, my scalp, my back - winding like an
ancient scarf around my neck, too tight, too close, too
familiar, reeking of old musk, that no washing can ever
get rid of

when I've had quite enough of that old scarf, it can go
down to the charity shop, where some much more
deserving soul can try it on for size.

I wish them luck.

Bare Knuckle Fight

I am teetering
around this rowdy ring
My heart is clattering
My fists are clamouring
to stop this tottering
and feel his sting

Yellow corner stares out
Red corner glares out
I throw out a dare pout,
I'm set to square off
and fight
out of this ring

Ding! Ding! The bell brings it!
He hammers his fist
to batter me first
He cannot resist! Now at last
I can win
Yes. Yes. I desist.

I was teetering
about this wedding ring
but with no smattering
of remorse
I cast it off.

Nausea

nausea comes at the damnedest times

in bed
after feeling nothing
it slammed me in the stomach
hurled a rock right into me
twisted up my core
sent out waves of sweating shock
i could not wrench it out

seasickness at least can be relieved
as you heave your guts up over the side
and the agonies of birth
are lost to puking up your pride
and that ghastly swirling-round-the-room
that comes   after *one too many*
makes me queasy just to think
about a drink

But this?

this

is the nausea
when you tell your partner
'It is over'
your deed devastates

9/11 crashes centre
and you leap
but later on, in bed as your body slips
into exhausted sleep
an emotional explosion
retches up
to make you weep

an unexpected chundering
thundering through your core
like you'd parachuted bodily
and you're bloodily left raw

it's nausea
so physical   so sickeningly stuck
that relieving it
by heaving
it up

oh fuck

Hill of the Dead

She laid me to waste on the Hill of the Dead
Where vultures swooped down, till my writhing fell
still
Razor, pale eyes, sharpened and flicking, cast
Clawing cruel beaks to rip out my bleak will

She laid me to waste on the ripe paddy fields
Where nightmarish dreams tramped down my sweet
life
Her sickle, it sliced, it rose, and it fell
Devastation she reaped, my brazenfaced wife

*

piercing the silence of the hill
cavorting up the emerald fields
a brightly swaddled groom and bride
come by   a-dancing

silk and saris shimmering
virulent golds and greens
shivering the breezes
before the monsoon rains

skipping by oblivious
their dance so joyful
lusty blind
callous and careless of my pecked-out corpse
and hollow, empty, dying eyes

their fluttering
red and purple passions
prancing in time with the vultures' wings

my hacked out being, laid to rot, feels
nothing.
nothing.
nothing.

*

But my beloved India
Who'd never let me leave her long
The brothers too, despite their warring
Carry me back home

There, in wracking anguished grief
They tend my jagged wounds
And bandage me into a pyre
And cleanse me with its living flame, so I should rise
again

*

My wife in white knelt by my side and stricken, wept
her shame
Her tears so salty, sati deep
The Ganges River sourced and flowed
To purge dead souls who sleep

And naked by the Washing Ghats
The waters flow yet, wide and slow
My life, my children, and my wife now, borne along
Not one letting another go

Bittersweet

A wanton loving frolic
can strengthen your systolic
But when you're acting diabolic
it can end up vitriolic

Oh!

Life's bittersweet

Thus

She walked out of the front door
Her children calling after her
A rucksack slung so casually
On her shoulder told the truth

This would be the last time
She'd walk out as a wife
The first step of a journey
Thus! She left behind her life.

Flying outbound from a place
Hard frozen by the snow
Leaving there a married face
When old, she'd never know

Miles skimming silently
beating a retreat
Sedan chair plane-seat
bearing her upon her wing-ed feat

Greeting her so tenderly someone she thought she knew
He and she preparing to start their lives anew
The lovers sauntered arm-in-arm under soul-mate skies
By seas of radiant aqua blue reflecting back their eyes

They hugged and kissed in sultry air
But soon, too soon, the air turned chill
Although she knew he loved her still
Their sweet heartbeat fell ill

For three decades each had wondered
Where each other was
But when it came to meet and care
Their love turned sour in balmy air

Time had left their feelings torn
Both had grown apart too young
And thus, she left behind her life
But never a seed was sown

Two-way Glass

Two-way glass in secret hotel
Behind the glass and looking out
Quiet observer misses nothing
In stealth he watches guests arriving
Knowing later they will pay him

Guests set down and get drawn in
He can make them feel at home
Every need is carefully tended
Wine and lunches, warmth and comfort
The management's always there

For room service, dial the number
Arriving now right to your door!
A trolley full of sweet confection
To tempt you even more
(But oh yes, you'll pay later)

For some the stay is pure contentment
Some rest a long while, whilst others go
Some get dependent on the service
Dreading leaving, leaving crying
While paying up their secret bill

All the while behind the mirror
The manager with stealth and cunning
Watches every guest depart
And that's because he's calculating
Precisely how   to steal their heart

Let Down

You let me down, you bastard!
What happened to all we said?
The whispered dreams, the cloudless sky,
a brand-new home, a life in bed!

You let me down, you bastard!
Why did you let me think
that you could be so good for me?
That we could be a family?

You let me down you bastard!
I just wanted a chance
to plug the gap left in my heart,
to be with you, make a new start!

But

You let me down, you bastard!
And now we are

Apart.

The Sigh

i drag in a sigh - releasing it hard
the sound of disappointment
is a sad lonely one   heard by only one

the sigh skulks in my breast
prowling beast cannot rest
there's no hunting a Snark
while this brute leaves it mark

i drag in a sigh - it claws deeper this time
the sum of disappointment
is a sad lonely one   scored by only one

once the world offered hope
and a life full of feeling
but it wasn't to be
it was there for the stealing

i drag in a sigh - releasing it hard
the dismay of disappointment
is a sad lonely one   exhaled by only one

he gazed in my eye, then grabbed my good day
all hope of sincerity, passion and sighs
were crushed and then trashed
and then spat out as lies

i drag in a sigh - releasing it hard
the stab of disappointment
is a sad lonely one   felt by only one
and that's me

Missing-part Life

i miss 'hello you'
when you open the door to me
your sun-awake smile
and your comforting tea

i miss your passion,
your flaws and even your fury
your tender-touch fingers
and your brow, when you're weary

i miss your sharp chat
and the depth of your voice
your rapt concentration
and your world-wise advice

you unwrapped the soul in me
made love to the heat of me
you completed the jigsaw
of my missing-part life

and I still love you

The Void

The Void and
i
sit
alone
i
hear
my
own
mute
beat
retch
at
my
heart
sick
heat
smell
my
sweat
stale
skin
taste
why's?
lip
sting

please   touch
me
so
we
can
be
one
hear

me
or
i
will
be
gone
see
me
or
thy
will
be
done

please   just
reach
me

before the Void and i become one

Canine Crater: haikus for my dog I

cold rug, empty house
lead limp as a hangman's noose
sets your silence loose

no one sees this chasm
this canine crater of loss
where once rolled rapture

come summer you leapt
come autumn you scattered leaves
come winter   you slept

Acetylene

the burbling blanket of bath-time
swaddles her and lulls her flesh
warm, oily, fragrant
lapping rocking
enticing her below its steamy depths
humid air, tropically tranquil
draws pause as
her acetylene soul
solders with the
sea of tranquility
bless'ed stream and river still

yet her sallow eyes
reflect a solitary well

all laughter lost
her level lists
her soul's embrace
so misses his

she sinks her lovely face
and rusty wrought iron wrists
beneath the
silent mists

and sleeps

Magnitude I

The end when it comes is not as I'd have imagined it…

I crack the seal on the draught we've all been sent.
I believe I am the last…

The world made its preparations, the virus spreading
rapidly, its magnitude unseen

The authorities informed us, 'Wash your hands' they
said. 'Wash your hands'. But offices and schools shut
down, utilities would be last, with the broadcasters

We all had to stay inside, from widows to newly-borns.
But too little was too late, a bat had got its own back for
our global greed

We stayed within our families and sang 'Oh! Happy
Birthday, Happy Birthday to you …Happy Death day to
you' and we clapped the NHS after the final curfew

The Internet of Things and our mobile phones were
charged. We said we'd try to share the end – but no,
that didn't last. The Internet coughed up its best, though
there was nothing new – just the words 'global
pandemic' and   mawkish adieux.

Once we'd Skyped our kids in Australasia that was it.
Masque balls became the silence of the lambs

We'd stored up food and drink, stockpiled for months
ahead. In the end,   our end,   it will be eaten by the
ants.

The end when it comes is not as I'd have imagined it…

Nothing   but bird song.

I draw the draught to my lips… and drink.

Poems of Love & Hope | **Mountains**

Hope's Genesis

lying chilled amid the snowdrops

peaty soil assails her senses

she stretches feline

as winter sun restores and strokes her

the stormy darkest night

her bed a scant-dug den

she barely held together

as wild beasts inhaled her

but now her spirits, soaring like winsome kites

illuminate hope's genesis

her muscles sense reviving dawn

and their tensions relent

Woman

Woman
Where are you going?
Is this whalebone arch your prison?
Do you trudge the shadowed steps of time?
Or is this walk a path of treason?
Does it trip your jagged edge of reason
and swallow up your rhyme?

pacing through life's mouldering hours
breathing in its mildewed walls
my black and white of good intention
seems shrouded by the muted calls
of thwarted hope and veiled reflection

Woman
Did the silken fall of child-like footsteps
Skipping sunshine, missing shade
So soon become a weighty tread
When burdened by where your life led you
And the load you bore with sickened dread?

my shadow seeks to skulk beside me
no light appears in this drab tunnel
no starry night seeks to inspire me
i see no end to this bleak channel
there's only darkness – not a view

Woman.
Bear the rawness of your shoe
Stroll with wonder through the stillness
Wring out sungleams from the gloom
Face the night and paint the stars!
Walk with Courage. Banish Doom

And Woman
May I walk beside you?

Spinoza Spirits

all colours grey
sunlight ghost white
heart fills up
empties out
days full hollow
future gone

thought life was kind   but

i walk
i sleep
i read

i find philosophy of times before
and learn a hope that balms despair:

Spinoza spirits gone from us
inspire choice in all our lives
so now at last I trust
when passions' prison doors release

we'll dance as one!
and what is to be, will be
and come

and pass

And Sunshine Helps

remember
the heart jewels
you take from fair isles
don't sweat the small
stuff or even the big
dying and grief
are all part of life
accept them and cry dear
cry hard
we carry our loved ones
Māori exhale their life breath
and inhale them in *hongi*
magic exists
goodwill surrounds you
money's no matter if you
think rich
you will be
human kindness is free
always asks to be shared
be true to yourself
and be good to others
if you radiate love
it comes back

and
sunshine helps

Tuesday Lunchtime

what a strange Tuesday lunchtime

a slaying quake
a tumbling Tasman ice and spires
fire plumes
streets spewing wires
and smoke and screams and bodies
kind of Tuesday lunchtime

Oh Aotearoa!

you face your darkest day
gentle accents calming terror
in a city set in *God's own*
as blood and fear
bear war-zone horror
on the evening news

the Richter scale strikes *Devastation*
liquid sidewalks bubble, swirling
surging waves send sirens wailing
horns and humans yell for help
beneath
the death-quake rubble

Damn you Ring of Fire!

you slaked your thirst!
you turned jade grass to hellish shards
shock fractured earth and brick and glass
and buried children of the world
and babies of five weeks

But just one thing

you picked a fight with mortals' best
folks of heart and kindest kin
who aren't too keen on giving in

for Kiwi grit is strong as steel - a humane spirit of
goodwill
that won't be overcome
by one strange Tuesday lunchtime.

Venez May Day

Three pebbles thrown into a bull-reeded pond
Slowly sink down, lost in tangles beyond

Should I follow their path, abandon my own?
Let weeds drag my day down, till fish pick my
bones?

Ephemeral fingers claw round from behind
Taunting my mayday and chilling my mind

A look in the eyes of a child not quite sure
A yagging like toothache, a lurking crow's craw

Furrows of doubt, should I stay, should I go?
Plough my distress, a quagmire of yes/no

A shrilling church bell laughs aloud for the dead
Piercing my musing and turning my head

I gaze at a mayfly which lives for one day
It lives so it may fly and flies just to lay

Through my anguish and doubt, it awakens my heart
Which knowing itself, beats from still with a start

So, I gather my hackles and vanquish my dread
Damn! I'll celebrate May Day, for I'm not yet dead!

Woodland Walk

Damn you!
Let me go!

Let me walk away
My back dismissing you
My strides strong
and lion fierce

Let *you* thoughts stop racing
Let them find a contemplation bench
Only then, can I quench
this thirsting, heaving, headlong rush
into wretchedness!

Let me wrench your lark-sweet song from my ears
your landscape looks from my eyes
your butterfly touch from my skin
your iron-man essence
from my being

Let me stand redwood tall and cypress strong
A wall.
A heath-stone heavy senses guard
where once there lay your gently tender open hand
on the stepping stile between us

Let me strike you from my sapling's core
and plunge a deep, serrated felling saw
into your bursted blister bough
to still the sap that sears my veins
And make you feel my might!

Let me go!
Damn you!

Our woodland walk
is done

Love's Sunrise

in love's sunrise

pits of loneliness
light
with
friends

anger's glaciers
yield
to
floe

captive touch is
freed
by
kisses

and open arms
fell
Jericho

Ocean's Drop

i caught you in my mirror
and knew you instantly
your face endeared by kindly time
still made you known to me

within that ocean's drop
when atoms meet and touch
we shared an elbow-hugging joy
elation plumped our clutch

our chatter flickered out, like light
as we melted candle truths
old moon arose to jest with breeze
whose breath caressed our youth

my rapture brushed your cherry lips
and sought to silk your skin
and soon i couldn't hear your words
for their honey drew me in

Essence

sweet honey love you stilled my lips
your lightness filled my eyes
your letters lulled my reverie
and our essence came alive

azure-sky eyes opened wide
but fate decreed our worlds divide
tender hearts were cast aside
and our essence crept inside

yet now our hearts' heat balms our cold
let the winter's world grow old
heaven's hope is brave and bold
we found our essence still survives

Reclining on a Bench

reclining on a bench
by the sea
two companions
side-by-side
take the air of
eventide and
affability

then arm in arm
we stroll the beach
and talk of
you and me
while celestial moon clouds
scud the sands of
compatibility

as sandy sunset
yields to
platinum lunar sea
two minds entwine
to stem the tide of
time's trickling
eternity

Relentless

Letters
Post-cards
Emails
Texts
|
Office
Lifts
A kiss
The Rex
|
Longing
Thinking
Yearning
Aching
|
Buzzing mobiles
Darkest dawn
'Not long to wait love - sunrise soon'
|
'Say something nice'
'I miss your love'
'I want your sex'
'I need your warmth'
|

|
Nights
Days
Wrong
Right
|
Showers
Swims
Gyms
Squash
|
Working
Driving
Sleeping
Typing
|
Other men
Other mothers
Other lives
Other lovers
|
Always loving
Always living
Always lying
Never leaving
|
Buzzing mobiles
Darkest dawn
'Not long to wait love - sunrise soon'

Gently

when all this is over
i'll stroll with you
through sun-hatted lanes
as gently as escaping dandelion rains

when all this is over
i'll lull with you
on peony-plump beaches
as gently as sun-drowsing waves

when all this is over
i'll unfurl my honest skin with yours
under dawn-dappled sheets
as gently as morn-waking snowdrops

when all this is over
i'll scroll my quiet breath with yours
in ear-humming pine-tree peace
as gently as the sweetening breeze

Philosophy Falters

Why are you smiling?
Because I love you

tender touches   breaths as one
velvet angel arms surrounding
bold wings folding loved one in

lighthouse peaceful, silence, golden
lips and breasts and skin on fire
heart invading

Come on darling, we are good, be proud not shy

in a moment
philosophy falters
chemistry conquers
occupation is inevitable

Are you ready?
Yes. I am

tsunami waves surge unsurpassed
sweetest heat relieved at last
sky-blue eyes reflecting black
euphoric rapture smiling back

a reef for waves dispelling fear
surrender sometimes harbours tears

It's okay
I've got you
got you
got you

two as one, both spirits shining
heaven's haven   holding   binding

Why are you smiling?
Because I love you. Yes. I love you

The Spring

out of obscurity into the light
a small and sparkling spring arose
bubbling unseen to the surface
clicquot-clear and wonder full

come winter

the fattening droplet wobbled her way
down rocky mountain sides
until giggling at her own instability
she   found   her   ground
and slid into a meander
through fields and hills in curls and curves
passing verdant pastures by
and lamb-ling lovers wandering

come spring

meander swelled into a proud and
sensual river, flowing fuelled
with ease and grace
blossom full, matriarchal
the large expectant river slowed
sailing proud and weighty by

come summer

gurgling green unseen and gasping out her last
a dull and dark most slender fall
trickle crept back into pasture
dripping down through rocks unseen
power lost, less than a stream
she slid and fell in silent glide
into dank caverns' gloom

come autumn

trickle felt new water fall
her force, full-fountain wet and thrusting
bursting out with urgency
rushing out with sparkling sound
spring danced with swirling sea
where all through relativity in water wide
and space and time   they would at last
be free

One Day

never be afraid to try

employ effort, diligence,
patience, care

life is short
failure no indignity

stay true to yourself
and one day

you will achieve
great things

The Breath Connects Us

at four you breathed me in
inspired to know my baby skin
my inhales then unknown to me
as oxygen for living in

you breathed me in

i breathed you in
before i breathed in mama's tears
and dada's darkness
and dust of ashes

i breathed you in

and still i breathe
so many breaths since then
and as i do the breath connects us
each one joins me up to you

you breathed me in

i took my first breath
i breathed you out
you gasped your last
but still i breathe — the breath connects us

Fibonacci

It's a boy! Oh, joyous cry!

Screams primeval now abating

Soon replaced by kitten mewling

Mews of *milk* from curled up comfort

                  Loud and urgent to maternal ears

Mouth meets breast – volcanoes surging

Pinprick sparks – womb home withdrawing

Vents erupting, magma melting

New life, cast from past is clinging

              At last!   Life starts anew

Mouse-dormant sweet curled Fibonacci

Under watchful mother's eye

With ashen heart for this new lover

Should she wake him, touch him, hold him

              or leave him be to sleep the night?

Joy

Elation must have filled your mother's heart,
As with you cradled in her arms, she felt
Such bliss, such love-plumped charms to name you Joy
her source of wonder, pleasure and delight

Gossamer girl, topaz eyes, saint-silk hair and sunrise smiles
Your youth a blur of war-torn Blitz and loss
Yet never did you lose your sweet, clear sight
Nor carefree air of wonder, pleasure and delight

Your soul mate looking in a window
where Rapunzel threw her hair down
Cast a passing word and hoped you would be
his true source of gladness, rapture and delight

And soon 'I do' was whispered to the knight

But the Reaper came to visit you one day
When snow lay on the ground
Your own small boy just lent to you
And sorrow tore your tower down

But a cradled baby helped you through.

And this curly head, she found in you
a Magna Mater - a decay-defying
Desiderata and her own eternal
fount of wonder, pleasure and delight

Elation fills your daughter's heart,
as with you cradled in my arms, I feel
Such bliss, such love-plumped charms to call
you Mum
My own life source of wonder, pleasure and
delight

Dark Skies

Chestnut hair and storm-grey eyes
But Nan was born neath darker skies
Boots were marching   men were digging
Trench-coat soil   their graves for dying

November days brought forth Nan's Joy
A baby girl in her arms lay
Her child's pure and calm love flowing
Nan watched her only future growing

A decade on   jackboots were marching
Now neath planes and blitzkrieg bombing
Yet in Joy grew faith, love, hope
And eyes that watched her mother weep

One night, the two clung neath the table
Praying oak might halt the rubble
Still a bomb fell square and blew my grandpa
Splitting heads and spewing blood

But as homes collapsed, with sirens ringing
A small voice rose in valiant singing
And neath dark skies of war's upheaval
A tender child song vanquished evil

Dancing Daughter

flowing flaxen hair
the hues of turning oak leaves
skeins of spider silk
swirl around you like friends

waving and skipping
upon sunny autumn breezes
your cob-grass eyes reflect
the Queen of Camelot

dusky dainty beauty
wafting scents of summer
you skip on scudding clouds
through the orchards of your life

your arms in pirouettes
entwined within your ringlets
are hugging up my winters
like mothers of the world

and so, my darling daughter
as you glide collecting reasons
i'll observe you from the shade
as we both dance through our seasons

Trembling Twelve-ling

my trembling twelve-ling
crying tears from the heart
you fear that you anguish alone
and unheard

lost and not found
unsure of your part
you cut yourself off
to conceal your hurt

distance feels safer
though you're yearning to give
to the ones we both know
will always hold love

your foundations are stronger
than you realise
banish your sorrow
and lift up your eyes

your mother adores you
but her heart's full of grief
for the fury she bore you
though it was but brief

with us both full of guilt and of pain
feeling bad
though it's fine to be angry love
please   don't go to bed sad

Different

I am
not sad
not bad
not mad
just different

I am
not scum
not numb
not some
just different

I am
not blind
not deaf
not dumb

just different

Just different to you

Locusts on Holiday

imperceptible dark specks, snaking hypnotically, swelling,
creeping, crawling, falling… a rising, billowing, buzzling
bubble of monstrous, marauding, munching mouths… just
swallowing, sucking, fattening, frightening fiends
called
LOCUSTS!

Malaria, Tetanus, Typhoid, Cholera
Fear of flying, ice on the wings
Take-off turbulence, bumpy landings
It's *Holiday Subcontinent*
With joyous breathing in's!

Daring driving, endless over-taking
Humanity in buses, on bicycles and taxis
Advancing Ambassadors, rickshaws and elephants
Walking or riding
But the
LOUDEST HOOTER WINS!

'*Om…*'

Crystal clear waters secreting bacteria
Seductive swimming pool – but it leads a double life
Infinity's chlorinity obscuring the jeopardy
of mirror-lake glass slivers
That will slice you like a knife!

Oh no!'

Cut toe, bleeding
Dripping on the patio!
Hobbling out crying, patted and piggybacked.
'Hold on a sec… just while I clean it.'

'Ow!'

'Should we stitch it, leave it or tape it?'
'One thing is for sure, mate: no swimming now.'

'Waaah!'

Don't drink the water!
It harbours unknown germs!
Don't brush your teeth in it or swallow any worms!
Low-squat toilets, with a bucket and a tap
Better just to take a pee, than risk having a c… p!

Watch out for mozzies they can take a fatal bite
Chikungunya, Dengue Fever,
You'll be scratching it all night
But Malaria is scarier
So, use the cream! Alright!

'Om…'

Trying to sleep in our quivering, moonlit temple
A frail, hallowed haven for our pampered lives
Anxieties engulf us like swarming plagues of locusts
Consuming calm within their path
And dishing desolation with their eyes

Malaria, Tetanus, Typhoid, Cholera
Fear of flying, ice on the wings
Take-off turbulence, bumpy landings
And
time to
pack our
bags for
home
With joyous breathing in's!

'Om…'

Birches

birch leaves kissing cyan skies

shiver me back home

where apple pie sits steaming

The Beach

I have always loved the beach where

speckled shells clinging like twins

some cut in half or cracked and broken

paint white spatters upon the tan volcanic sands

evading time and giving succour to

dried out grasses who looking dead belie their strength

as they assume a casual air

waving and wafting and signalling to

sea terns hanging effortlessly upon the breeze

languorously lilting and lurching till they dive into the

frothing waves where darting diamond whitebait swim

in shoals attempting hard to seem

bigger than they really are within

the sea's aqua marine reflecting back

the sparkling sun

in all its summer glory

I have always loved the beach where

waves slap gently and sometimes splash onto the

sucking sandy shoreline where

scuttling crabs post popping bubbles as they run to

hide their shyer side from

cawing predatory gulls flapping their wings before

cracking shells upon the rocks to find inside

frothing cockles whose only home gets left and

falls onto the running sands whose

whipping winds across the vast expanse

get trapped without a murmur inside the smoothest

holes of driftwood there making liquid shapes among

jurassic rocks where slapping waters come to

while away all time through ebb and flow

as the moments wash on by

Gold of Ages

hands held skipping, running, cartwheels
beaches
boats
and sunrise shared
the golden gaze of carefree childhood
Friends forever! Never scared!

You got something that I wanted!
envy
pouts
and insults shared
these things in life were sent to rent us
But it's only stuff. Who cares?

whispered gossip, minus malice
Sorry
shrugs
and coffees shared
I really never meant to hurt you
Forgive me?

arms held nursing, eyes with love in
wonder
bliss
and bathtimes shared
our children's games renew our bond
their laughter keeps it aired

arms held grieving, eyes with pain in
mounds of
earth
and mourning shared
I never thought this day would come
I feel so   unprepared

yielding hugs gift words unspoken
acceptance
hope
and journeys shared
Sister, I will never leave you
One blood flowed; our fingers paired

wealth is knowing gold of ages
kindness
love
and firesides shared
one priceless element sustained us
our friendship's precious strength endured

The Swan: elegy for a dance teacher

There was once a beautiful dancing swan - whose extraordinary grace was seen by every creature on the wide river by the city. As she grew in beauty, she found a handsome mate like no other and their love grew stronger than the source of the water itself.

Travelling together, the tide of their love drew small birds to drink alongside them and soon a fluttering chorus followed their meandering way.

Young mallards, herons, starlings and peewits hopped and chirruped in the riverside reeds alongside the waltzing swans, who became as a mother and a father to each one.

The swans took their uncanny brood under their wings, raising their baby hops and flaps with caring guidance, until growing in confidence, each bird danced and sang and flew.

The birds loved the swans in return and feeling their feathers sparkling in the summer sunshine they sensed the pure light reflected in the river by them.

But one day, the beautiful dancing swan - whose extraordinary grace was seen by every creature on the wide river by the city - tumbled down a waterfall and her light was lost from view.

At her stillness, all the birds raised a chorus of lament so sad that snow fell, and the river turned to ice and ceased to flow.

Her heart-broken mate never left her side.

All her birds watched and waited. Distress pumped in their breasts all winter, until one spring dawn when the sun lifted across the snowy waters and rose-petals streaked the skies.

Out of the cool mists a beautiful shimmering swan took flight - whose extraordinary grace was seen by every creature on the wide river by the city - the beat of her snow-white wings caressing the air and warming it until the ice melted and the waters flowed again.

As they watched, all the courtiers of the riverside sang out loud to their Queen and knew that whenever they danced or sang or flew, they would ever after be following in the wake of an angel.

Hands

my fingers cast rainbows in ballet slow motion
rising like sunshine to stain-glass the sky

once these were tips that were rose-tender soft
catching sweet bridal bouquets thrown aloft

inquisitive digits exploring, imploring,
holding   enfolding   undressing   caressing

these hands that scribed pages of words unexpressed
are the same that lulled babies who lapped at my breast

exhaling, while opening the fingers i'm following
i'm watching my lifeline passing me by

gnarled, nodding knuckles, paper-thin skin
dapple-dotted freckles to engrave old age in

dry swollen thumbs, desert-sandpaper thick
join the maps on my palms, as parched as the quick

and these hands now in repose and mulled meditation
will soon rest in prayer pose and calm contemplation

Mousehole in May

Gone too soon dear friend,
the gash of loss beyond profound

No words ease grief's rawness, only thanks for dear days, the
last at Mousehole in May, now a pebble-
palming memory, where we walked and we talked and
you cooked us one last supper

You lived your life to the full and your passion,
commitment, curiosity and love left the world a better place.
Your legacy of photographs still feeds us
life through your eyes

Your laughter's echoes cradle the pain, so too your
garden gifts of veg and flowers, soon to
rise, through earth and rain

But for now, we'll hug your family to our hearts for
you, and love them in your absence. In three fine sons
you will live on

Their tears, wet or dry, reflect their love for you and yours
for them
And not for a moment, a life wasted

Believe

when your dad talked about you
i looked at your photo
i soon recognised you
the son of my friend
an enquiring gaze
a faithful coal tousle
obscuring a shyness
i'd known long ago

when i first got to meet you
i was nervous as hell
and i made you turn tail
with my mad zealous hound!
but time forged a nexus
and respect replaced caution
and you dished out raw talent
and on-key syncopation

you're a new Prince of Pride
your king skulking inside
is preparing his mark:
a significant deal - a unique sonic spark
so, your friends list keeps growing
just like me, they sense something
never fear where you're going
with the gifts you'll bestow

believe in yourself
always trust your gut feel
leave the doubters behind you
and embrace your strong will
be sure of your truth
you can reap what you sow
just believe in yourself

In this   trust me
I know

Canine Crater: haikus for my dog II

freedom was my dog
               ever flowing through green fields
                             and sandy beaches

gratitude soothes me
               knowing we both loved our best
                             two lives crossed and blessed

joy bounding the green
               ever pounding out your love
                             for me, my dear dog

On Solitude

loving kindness soothing anxiety meditation.   i am
surrounded by all the angels of my life,   not alone
the love they imbue me with is greater than any   i am
able to feel in this world. they are all there,   not
just to my right, but beyond me, all those, when   alone
i've loved and known, they encircle me   now,
angels all, angels all. no   i am not alone
i just couldn't see it until   now

I Breathe In

I breathe in air so full of promise
a milkshake-misty morning sky
lures me out to mountain forests
padding past saplings, cowslips and fox holes
coo-cooing pigeons woo me through

first strides feel dense - and strained.
I labour.
Free me! scream ribs as my breathing slows
in-out, in-out, beating-a-rhythm
breathing-in, keeping-in,
time-with-my toes

my heaving heart is clockwork now.
trudging up a steep incline
petty grasses beat me back,
my muscles feel so flimsy frail
Oh! Damn this hill! Don't let me fail!

feeling stronger, bounding paths
past friendly farmers' winter-feeds
and kindly leafy canopy
on across the valley ridge until
a panoramic panoply of hills   spills   out

the final run is all downhill
I hear my breaths and ear-blood pounding
sweating top lip, steps rebounding
just keep going past the neighbours
pride, before exhausted fall!

I glimpse me looking from a window
rosy cheeks and glittering gaze
Ah! Bliss has come in with the run!
my glistening skin and fulfilled smile
show me the proof   a run's worthwhile

Love

with your love
cloaking my shoulders
all my homesickness leaves
for I come home

my hunger
feasts at your table
my thirst
laps up your words

my humour
delights in your smile
my spirit
warms itself by your fire

my soul
stills in your arms
and my voice
grows soft and calm

when you are with me
you fill me
you feed me
you find me

with your love
cloaking my shoulders
all my homesickness leaves
for I come home

I am home

Profound

i found you
the profound you
i surround you
and confound you

i free you
i feed you
i lead you
and i need you

you found me
the profound me
you surround me
and confound me

you free me
you feed me
you lead me
and you need me

and for all this darling
i thank you

Single Bed

the shadows fall
in a fanlight familiar way
as i drowse up
from groggy sleep

i'm in my parents' home
my childhood bedroom
where everything
feels safe and warm

light diffuses skin-soft
from the hallway
a loving beam to
kiss my nestling cheek

the bready burble
of ma and pa
watching television in the lounge
milk-comforting

my mind travels
through the home of
my heart and i realise
all the beloveds of my life exist there

in that single bed
in my childhood nest
where i see myself
snuggled safe among the shadows

Magnitude II

The end when it comes is not as I'd have imagined it…

Nothing   but bird song

I draw the draught to my lips… and drink

and all is well

Please Review

I breathe in: Poems of loss, love & hope

I hope this book of poetry resonated with you on many different levels. If so, please leave an honest review on Amazon and recommend your favourite poems, so others can enjoy them too.

Thank you for reading *I breathe in*.

Julie

About the Author

Julie Salt is a British writer and poet. *I breathe in* is her debut poetry collection, written over more than a decade and compiled after taking a Master's Degree in Creative Writing and Publishing at Bournemouth University, which she achieved with distinction. She has also written a novel - to be published soon.

Some of the poems in this book are based on true events in the poet's life, most notably the death of her brother when she was a baby. As a result, poems often take on a unique life of their own as facts merge with fiction to express hidden and universal 'truths'.

Julie was educated at a secondary modern school and a further education college in Poole, Dorset. She took a Bachelor's Degree in English and Drama at Aberystwyth University and later trained as a Radio Journalist at the London College of Printing. In 1987, she achieved her dream to join BBC TV and Radio News as a Broadcast Journalist and worked over the years for *BBC Radio Cambridgeshire* and *BBC Look East* (Norwich), as well as *BBC World Television, News 24* and *BBC Breakfast* in London, until 2006. During her career, Julie covered many news and current affairs stories, ranging from war to reconciliation and family rights to feminism. She was also one of the journalists on the founding production team to help win *BBC HARDtalk with Tim Sebastian* its first Royal Television Society Award. She also gave birth to three children during that time.

Since leaving the BBC, Julie has edited, the book *Come the Evolution* (2019)[6] by Nabil Shabka, attended Creative Writing workshops run by Oxford University's Department for Continuing Education and had articles and blogs published by magazines and newspapers, including *The Daily Telegraph*. In addition, she has advised on the short documentary *Death Café* directed in Christchurch, New Zealand by Austin Salt-Cowell, and taught journalism to students in Wellington, NZ and the UK. New Zealand continues to be a country close to her heart and features both in her poetry and forthcoming novel. Julie currently lives in the south of England.

Endnotes

[1] Battat Silverman, R., and Brenner, A. MD., 2015
Replacement Children: The Unconscious Script
Published by Sandhill review Press, San Mateo, CA.

[2] Battat Silverman, R., and Brenner, A. MD., 2015
Replacement Children: The Unconscious Script Pp.57-58.
Published by Sandhill review Press, San Mateo, CA.

[3] Emerson, R.W., 1880. 'Preface' In: *Parnassus:*
An Anthology of Poetry pp.22 Boston: Houghton, Osgood
and Company, New York. Available from:
https://www.bartleby.com/371/ [Accessed 05-05-2020]

[4] Pound, E., 1914. 'Vorticism' In: Fortnightly Review
NS 96. September 1914. pp. 461-71. Available from:
http://themargins.net/anth/1910-
1919/poundvorticism.html [Accessed 19-07-2019]

[5] Avia, T., 2016. 'I Cannot write a poem about Gaza' In:
Fale Aitu | Spirit House. pp. 75 Wellington: Victoria
University Press. NZ.

[6] Shabka, N., 2019. *Come the Evolution*. Independent
Publisher and 2nd edition published, 2020.
Available from: https://www.amazon.co.uk/
dp/B0849XGF4T/ref=rdr_ext_tmb [Accessed 13-05-2020]

Printed in Great Britain
by Amazon